Confessions to Dulcinea
And Other Poems

by

FRANK DALE

CONFESSIONS TO DULCINEA

ISBN # 978-1-7345872-6-5

INTRODUCTION

*M*y life has mostly been a preoccupation with the beauty of the human female. All other manifestations of beauty seem to me to be only an echo. According to my version of Webster's Dictionary: 1. 'Beauty' is the quality or aggregate of qualities in a thing which gives pleasure to the senses or pleasurably exalts the mind or spirit; physical, moral, or spiritual loveliness. 2. A beautiful person or thing, esp. a beautiful woman. 3. A particular grace, ornament, or excellence; anything beautiful; as, the beauties of nature.

There is it seems to me, a clearly profound vagueness, even by the dictionary, as to Beauty's nature. It seems to come very close to those kinds of answers people give when they are pressed beyond the bounds of language and they resort to: "I really can't explain it in words but I'm sure you'll know it when you you see it". I like to think of her and the way she affects me in much the same way I experience the manifestations of gravity; I can never hope to to explain or escape its power over me but I can express adinfinitum how it makes me feel and call it poetry if I choose.

If you care to know more about my thoughts on Beauty, you will find some clues in these few poems. Some of my favorite words describing her are "magic", "mystery" and "paradox"

CONFESSIONS TO DULCINEA

CONTENTS

FRANK DALE

CONFESSIONS TO DULCINEA

CONFESSIONS TO DULCINEA

CONFESSIONS TO DULCINEA I

Dearest Dulcinea,

This message long overdue in the writing and endlessly delayed by mortal combat, leaves me now both dismayed and grateful that it has at last found its way to paper and from there, with luck, to you. I cannot know how you will accept it, but I'll say in its behalf that its born of purest heartfelt truth and dewy solitude...enough to bear some lovely blossoms, though I think you may not have seen them. But that strays! (I think I see why the circular movement of the windmill so compels me. At least why some windmills turn madly in my mind. But I can safely say for all the angry winds and splintered pikes this is one pinwheel I'll bring to rest!)

No matter how you shall receive this, though I pray it be kindly, it is nonetheless only put to words what is truly true in the private portals of my heart, unshared 'til now. And so, here's my treasure; the jeweled memory made of pure and shining thought; my mind's record of something long since passed which, even so, grows clearer with each sublime recital.

Alone I close my eyes in quiet reverie and see...the evening sun slide past the window magically incandescing warm red tints hiding in your hair.....too soon the spectrum shifts...your glowing curls darken and softly go out of focus....the light of day pulls its purple curtain into the peaceful western sea...too little light for the eyes now...just right for the mind to see forever, to mix and savor the random wonders of pleated plaid and wool and warmth and touch and mouth and kiss...and kiss...and kiss...and ....oh.

Was it honey? I've always thought it so. Never again was there such a kiss. O' foolish man! Not ever! Did you think that every head's a hive and oozing sweet divinity? O' silly man! O' wondrous and willowy woman wherein honey kisses dwell how fare you there in the velvet corridors of my most cherished dreams? Are you well kept? Do you laugh and cry? Do we together share that forever flawless kiss? Can you ever speak to me of kissing? One thing's sure: I'll keep you kindly on my mind forever or as nearby it as I may come.

And so dear mellifluous Dulcinea, how was it I took leave of honeyed heaven to tilt at windmills? Was it courage, cowardice, perhaps fear? The truth lies quartered in there somewhere. It evades me still. But this I know full well: I'll always wish I had not left the sweetness that lies perfect in my mind.

I now fervent-fearful pray this heart spoke revelation brings you only private pleasure in the learning that you've been held

so dear...and yet to come awhile. O' Sweet Heaven, how I miss the kiss!
But dreams'll have to do. And there's still the matter of those damned windmills. I think I hear one now.
FD

CONFESSIONS TO DULCINEA II

Dearest Dulcinea,

The wonder of you is that you are there, alive and safe and unencumbered by the wanton exigencies of my daily sorties. Having survived from then 'til now, you're my inviolate principle, a fixed point, a banner proclaiming purpose and held aloft with a strength born of devotion to that purpose and the deep and burning love that one feels for such close and kindred souls. I surely love you past your knowing. How could I not? The thought of you has sustained me through fierce struggles and weary storms when all seemed lost and hopeless and nothing held me but the tender bond between us, like the thought of home to the tired traveler.

How so love, you ask? For what purpose and to what end? I'll tell you. Though, in some parts, there really seems to be no sense to it, it is never-the-less so that whatever drives a man to do-in dragons for the name of his lady, that thing is strong in me and drives me past all reason to its doing. What riddled paradox it is to chance the dice to not return at all and taste the love so daily won. I confess this logic has the smoothness, in gait, of a three-egged dog. But however strange it seems to sound there's some great truth and power in it, for I cannot make it halt or turn around. And so I'm here and you are there and I cannot say when I'll see your face again.... save in my dreams, which is where I think you really live.

Oh, the remembered warmth, the brimming full of love, the eternal memory of adoring and adored, the unforgettable touching of souls and lips separately and together, and every which way burning passion might direct.

I wish I could climb into your mind, you said that day so long ago. I never did tell you how that thought got stuck there; how it would pop up and bring a funny little smile to my face as I tried to visualize you taking off your shoe in preparation for creeping into my mind. It was, by all odds the most intimate and worshipful (notwithstanding the silliest) thing anyone ever said to me. I liked it so I made it to a banner which flies boldly from the mast of a well-rigged ship that plows alone the great solitary sea of my mind where none other dares to sail.

On nights like this, I just lie here, 'staring down' the stars, uncork my jugged-up dreams...my fancies...and drink my fill of you.

-FD-

CONFESSIONS TO DULCINEA III

Dearest Dulcinea,

I see December snow. Today is Christmas Eve. I've taken shelter from the cold. A day like this, without the Sun, I like to huddle by a fire and reminisce with dancing flames the times I spent with you: things you've said, the way you moved, how you looked, and how it made me feel. Just now I see the day I saw you last and that gnawing, awful emptiness that came upon me....that great foreboding, dark and dreary cloud. How I didn't want the clock to keep on counting...just dreaded leaving without seeing you again... one final time. I had too early said goodbye and enough formality had been tokened that I could hardly seek you out again and not disclose the weakness of my need...which I'd have surely shameless done if it might reveal to me the status of your heart. But something held me back...perhaps the fear to hear unwelcome news or just be left with vague uncertain thoughts to haunt my dreaming nights. Love like gifts, to me at least, must come freely given ....if the giving be believed, for wheedled love is not a thing to trust. So I was doomed to wait and see what time would tell and waited nervous on its tale. Inexorably, it just kept ticking on...my heart was like a candle burning down. I took serious council with myself and, defending you, insisted you'd behave impeccably. If things should go amiss, it would surely be my fault....this weakness I have fallen to...this terrible need I have for seeing you.

I prevailed enough in this, at last, and swore to bear the anguish should it come and promptly lost myself in things just needing to br done. When I heard a whispered sound and raised my head to see you standing there I was was thrilled and stunned at once. I had convinced myself not to expect you....so I might survive your not being there...in case you didn't come. Only when I looked into your shining eyes and saw the sensuous wonder of the fullness of your lips, which slowly parted in a smile, was I aware how choked and strangled were the muscles of my heart....for in that instant, when I finally grasped that you were there, such a peaceful joy came over me that only then did I understand how bad it would have been if I had left without seeing you again.

How merciful you were to know to come and save me. How can it be you always seem to know when desperation is so near? And when you put your arms around me and held me, oh so tight. I couldn't help but wonder, in that fleeing moment, if you might have guessed my secret...the terrible immenseness of my burning love for you.

CONFESSIONS TO DULCINEA

Your beauty's overwhelming! Even here, in this fearful frozen place, I think of you.... your sweetness...and feel the tears upon my face. Sleep well, sweet Dulcinea, I'll dream of you this cold December night.
-FD

CONFESSIONS TO DULCINEA IV
Dearest Dulcinea,

How unwelcome are the things that come between us! When you're out of sight upon my mind I have such a passion to find and hold you near, to feel your soft, firm body pressing close on mine, to slide my anxious fingers down the sensuous curving of your spine, then charge with bold and surreptitious daring to simply get the feel of you: to revel in the scented sable softness of your hair, to feel the measured breezes of your breath against my cheek, a shivered shudder shakes my arm as my frantic fingers find and fondly feel the erotic firmness in the fullness of your hips, then slyly slip to that mysterious small depression hidden in the narrow hollow of your back, from where they stage a dizzy climb, inching all the way, 'til at last, they reach the summit of your shoulders and rest caressing in the thicket of your curls, slowly, surely, smoothly, sliding, almost unnoticed, to lift so gently, the graceful oval of your chin...so I might, at last, gaze with loving wonder into the endless ebbing oceans of your eyes.

From this pinnacle, this peak, this tiny tip of time, to sway in balanced quandary: whether to risk the driven declaration of desire and open honeyed heaven's door or *tempt rejection's bitter fruit. So the burning question hangs there, blazing like the Sun, waiting for an answer yet wanting not to ask. Then to sense it, the grand and glorious 'yesness' shining somewhere out of you, never sure just what single thing it is...the beginning of a smile, a flicker of the eyes, an expanding kind of openness about your face, almost imperceptibly signifying a reaching, a longing....impossible to describe. Yet as clear and final as anything can be.*

Suddenly your lips are there and touching. Thoughts explode in blinding incoherent flashes: fragmented impressions; soft and tentative, warm and gentle, intimate and fuzzy,....clearly 'yes',...then drunkenly, 'yes' again but more...'Oh, yes', now, and then the sweetest sort of teasing, dreamily drifting with the tide, withdrawing, then, another surging wave comes rushing, reckless and engulfing as it goes,...'yes'...and finally that complete unqualified commitment,...a languorous, lingering, probing kiss where time stands still and bodies blend as one and nothing else exists in time or space except the burning promises that only kissing lips can say or hear, but loving minds will ever hasten to recall. Oh, sweet Dulcinea, may I live long enough to kiss you once again!

FD-

CONFESSIONS TO DULCINEA V

Dearest Dulcinea,

     A great storm now rages on this place and I'm uncertain I will ever see the Sun or Moon and stars again. But worse, I fear I may not look upon nor feel the warmth of you again except here in my heart and mind. I write these words in the fading hope that someone will send them to you if I should fail this ordeal. I always meant to tell you of the transformation, in me, which came from loving you. How much more I became and continue to be from knowing you. I see the world with more loving eyes because you love it. I hear sounds of birds, the wind, the rain and love them more because you are here inside me listening too. I revel in the 'unsound' silence of softly falling snow and feel you here beside me. You have magnified the beauty of everything. I live with two hearts.

     You have ended my loneliness while compounding it forever. Oh, sweet, Dulcinea, how can I ever make you know how desperately I adore you, how you make me shine. I can hardly bear the thrill of you sometimes, for fear of bursting my throbbing heart. I never knew such feelings before....and believed not anyone who ever claimed they had. I am without the power or means to convey to you the true depth of my feelings and yet I sputter and fume these pitiful words; knowing they fail... I fail to give to you anything like what you have given me.

There's a sad inequity here which I am gravely wounded by. I am a sword and you a rose, and there's a fine bouquet! Please, please, simply know this for all time, I love your heart, your soul, and your mind, more than anything that ever was or ever more shall be. Whatever keeps us apart will surely by my fault but not, Dear God, my wish that it should be. Adieu, Sweet Dulcinea, my love. Adieu.

FD

FRANK DALE

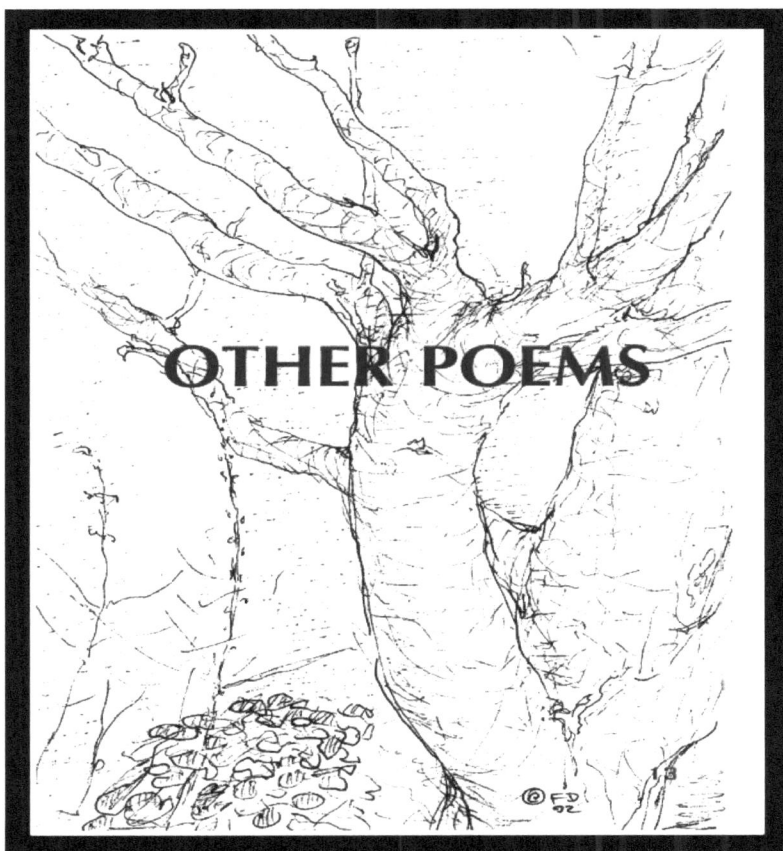

OTHER POEMS

TO AN EMPTY BOOK

You are nothing
'Til I'm done with you.
Your fields of white
Are empty sheets,
A place upon to woo
The love of my life.
And when I'm finished
Well, then we'll see
Just how good you are!
FD

SWEET WINE

Your poem is like wine...
Some rare vintage from
The sweet succulent fruit
That grows only on the sunny slope
Of a hillside up from a valley
Where morning dew
Sometimes hangs like tears
From the leafy vines.
I'm not sure the wine
Was mine to drink
But I drank it
Because I thought only I
Had been to that valley
And only I knew of those vines
And the sunlit slopes
And that teary dew,
But you have made this wine
With such loving skill
I see you have been there too.
I am now two days drunk
And drinking still.
When this intoxication's over
I'll sad despair the chance
To taste such wine again.
FD-

MARLA

Ben came in last night
With the legendary Marla in-tow.
I had my first encounter with her
(I spoke to her once on the phone).
She is tall and evenly splendid.
I was conscious of a new experience.
Like a tiger she is,
Full of deep fires
And fearless soft smiles.
Oh, the smoldering of her
Awed me into an unusual silence.
I just glanced at her
And made superficial pleasantries.
FD-

LEILANI

I spoke to her over the phone for nearly an hour and was completely awash with fanciful waves of exotic and blissful thoughts. I still hear her voice in my ears; the deep rich tones, the indomitable energy that rings clear and sharp. That loving and romantic soul still shines... no, blazes with mysterious convictions that were not lost when East met West and those genes found harmonies not often heard. I must see her and savor the loving strength of her. Oh, how full I am of yearning and desire, how now unafraid to be my age. This is new and peaceful. Oh, how rich, how sweet to be well and lovingly remembered from those days when I was young and full of promise and riding high! -
FD-

TO AN OSTRICH

O, sadness,
O, foolish unwisdom,
Bird with no wings,
What troubles your eyes that you see too much?
You held your head so high you thought you flew
But now the ground comes up at you
You've made lunacy an art
You just took a monumental fall
And I think you broke your heart.
You've got to learn this lesson soon
You're not a bird that gets a mate
And you never did, nor ever will,
Possess the sort of wings that fly.
FD-

CANDLELIGHT

I love the way a candle burns, its dancing drop of creamy light which waits so breathless on the air, not like some dainty bulb with its sheltered crystal glow, which though dependable, has just no sense of show.

A candle, on the other hand, is not afraid to take the risk and captivate your mind. A candle pops, will flop right down then zip up to a needle point, then lay some smoke and jump and chase itself around.

Unlike its wimpy, bubble-headed cousin, it can murmur on the wind. It can snap and sough like breezes through a pine, or lap and crack, then die right down to nothing...you'll think it's out. Then come roaring back and let you know it's just having fun. It duels the air and fights the wind and hardly ever gives right out.

The empty wind must blow and blow before it wins a bout...and even then a candle makes a splendid show; for when its flame is snuffed it spreads its ghost like angel dust and lets you watch the wind depart.
-FD-

DINING IN THE WOOD

I watched them for a moment. He sat like wood and stared at her. And she in silver specks and silver hair stared wooden back. I thought I saw a muscle move around his eye and after frozen time a twitch around his mouth. I couldn't hear from where I sat if any sounds were made, but then the food was brought, and they began to talk....at least her mouth engaged in constant changing forms. I strained but still could hear no sound.

But all was well for I could see him smile his wooden smile while she put on her wooden frown.

FD

THE WAITING WINE

The waiting wine, just waiting in the glass...waiting, with wanting held quite fast. Waiting...its promise held...to make it last. To know that when its tipped and tasted, the savored, fragrant, tingled thrill will slowly, surely, pass......be gone......no longer full of innocence-a-begging, but empty.......done and used forever.......and whatever might have been....is set in memory then and lives just in the past.

So where is there the best of it; as it's held.... with future promised, ...or does drinking, then remembering, really make it last? I'm not sure myself, but while I sit a bit and think on it, would you kindly pass the glass?

FD-

FARM GIRL

Sun drenched curls
Radiating profound and simple beauty
She belongs out of doors among the trees and grass.
A golden flower
With iron hands and will
She protects the living things she loves
As if the earth was hers
And must obey.
And so, it is.
And so, it does,
For she is not to be denied.
Still, beyond the unrelenting fierceness
Of her self-directed chores
There is tenderness without end.
No man can look into those all-seeing eyes
And not somehow sense
If she'd but let him see
And touch down deep into her soul
He...who is only ever half...
Might after all be whole
And might surely see then
Beyond all space and stars
Into infinity...
Oh, there'd be a life to live.
FD

FRANK DALE

NIGHT PASSAGE

My ship's alone afloat
Just drifting aimless through the night.
A foggy shroud engulfs the scene
Which falls within my sight.
I hear the slurping, slapping sea
That rocks me through the moonless night
To where I'm sure I've never been,
And may, in truth, never wish to be.
I pass eerie disembodied sounds
Of folks about their nightly coupled tasks
And still saw none
But only heard them
And felt some envy
As they made good cheer
And had no apparent care that
They were drifting...
Same as me.
FD

BEMUSED

Oh, soft and gentle creature
All lean and lovely there
I see such beauty wild within you
Beyond those huge bright eyes
Like doors to other worlds
What is this strange enchantment?
That I just sit and stare
And yet can hardly bear
The clear and empty space between us
My, how sharp both sides this sword can cut
That holds you out of reach
In order fully to be seen.
I may never solve the riddle
How to find you out across this endless room
And then again, how not.
Oh, No! Please don't turn and look away!
You must give me your permission
To search those dreamy caves
Where magic mystery lies hiding
Like great enormous spiders,
Spinning webs and weaving spells
To snare my helpless soul.
Why do I choose this curious exposure?
To bare myself and risk the chill?
Shall I ever understand it?
No, I doubt I ever will.
I'll just go, be lost and maybe die there
But I know I've got to go, to look, to see,
To find how Beauty sparkles,
What final atom makes her glow?

Or is my brain too small to think it,
My eyes inadequate to see.
I'm not sure just where this leaves me
But I'm certain I am captured
"Til Beauty sets me free.   FD

TIL BEAUTY COMES

At first, he thought 'twas Beauty
Come to save the Beast
But he was wrong, you see
Not this time, at least.
It was just the wind upon a tree
Banging branches on the wall
Will this torment ever stop?
Should he go on waiting for her call?
Time goes by and petals drop
And chances grow so small.
Now clouds grow dark,
A chill is in the air,
Soon rain will start to fall.
Is there any shelter here?
Anywhere at all?
Farewell sweet dream!
The precious time will soon be gone
There's nothing left it seems
But wait upon the ticking of the clock
'Til finally Beauty comes,
Or find, at last, that Beauty's but a myth,
A fairy tale, a dreamy thing,
A bit of childish fiction...
Nothing more, alas,
Alas, a lass
FD

RED ON YOU

To say that red looks good on you
Is to say that water's wet.
How small it stands in the shadow of the fact
Warm red cloth about your face, or neck, or arms
Strike a chord so resonant and rich
On the ears of my eyes
I tremble at the sight of the sound of it.
My mind's all eyes and thrills
And wordless dumb for the joy of red on you.
A red silk dress designed by my imagination
Would be all that red is for.
There'll be no further need,
Just an accent, a frame a background,
A perfect augmentation
For that ivory skin, the umber hair,
The deep dark waters of your eyes.
Oh, how infinitely edgeless
Are the pieces of it all,
The spectral majesty of red on you.
FD

A TOUCH OF GREEN

I was almost certain I was late. I raced along the hall. My thoughts were miles ahead when something green and very soft appeared from nowhere and was there within my startled grasp. No time to think, my arms had just reacted when my eyes saw something move. My hands and legs and feet didn't have to check-out with my brain, they'd been there before and knew exactly what to do.... dance a bit but don't fall down, and don't get someone hurt. It was over in a nano-second and I found myself reconstructing, with connoisseuring relish, each tiny well-placed move. How swift and sure my hand had closed upon the thing, the sudden sleeve of green, how in that micro-moment my mind was filled with falling things; the cloth was warm and soft and I think even felt the color green...this was all electric, nice to know, but it was nothing next to what was covered by it, the living thing inside, the tender trembling tissue, the well-proportioned bones, the myriad facts and fancies my fingers told my mind were true.

Dear God, my mind was running over with the thrill of touching you! Where did all this come from? How could I think so much so fast? What flashed this yearning through me? Did it come from there? Or was it just some kind of echo from the pounding of my *heart? I know there's something in there, something wonderful and wild, yet soft and gentle too. I think it's all I've ever dreamed of....has Beauty come at last? Has finally come to save me?*

"Have a care", I told myself. I think you walk too fast! But having stirred this sleeping phantom I knew there'd be no sleep tonight. And then, the crisis over, safe passage quite assured, all was well and done with. Then one half-beat past the needing that soft exquisite touch, that angel hand on mine, that second wave of feeling that swelled and broke and washed against my soul and held me so enraptured I nearly missed... a word was spoken...the gentle calling of my name. Oh, my, what dreams I gave! I know this never happened I just wished for it to be. My mind tries hard to please and conjures up this stuff for me to see. Anyone with half a brain knows that you can't feel the color green.

FD

TANGLED YARN

I felt a tiny tug, but I just let it pass. Then another came, then three, then four and then some more. And so I turned, at last, to find what made this rhythmic nudge. With pure surprise, I found you standing there. That impish angel look disarmed mu startled stare and I saw the warming smile and felt your tender velvet touch and knew in a surge of sudden joy ...you'd just been teasing me! And then I stood and bathed myself as love poured from your eyes. Oh, how sweet this playful purring, kitten-thing you are. You wanted something...which I got for you...and I held on to the time it took, as precious as it was, until at last I had to let you go. I couldn't stop it though I wanted to....to just be there and next to you. But off you went, and I back to my task.... with thoughts of you still tugging at my mind. How soft you are! To think of gently stroking from your head all down your back, until your eyes squeeze tight and then blink at me and I hear that rapt, purring sound, sends ecstatic shivers down my spine. Oh, how fine you are to cuddle to!

I confess, you do astonish me! Do you have the slightest clue, how warm you make me feel when I am next to you? I used to be, perhaps too sad, but even so, well-ordered in my days, (though lacking much in charm), and then you came by, with your kitten ways, and turned my life into a joyful, grinning, giddy, mess of tangled yarn.

FD

MOONLIT MEADOW

O, dear sweet, lovely love, last evening past I strolled my meadow by the stars. The Moon was there and so were you. You came and knelt by me and we trailed our fingers in a stream. Creeping close a cricket chirruped and further down we heard a 'ribbet' of a frog. The evening air was warm, a breeze up from the south, the water cooled our fingertips and burbled on its way while up above the smiling Moon found cotton puffs with which to play.

We wandered barefoot up a narrow path, puffing dust between our toes, until we reached a warming stone. We stayed the longest time just staring at stars. Touching some and talking some beneath that bowl of endless blue. Our talk was that of simple things, some was that of life, but mostly that of love....so it was I had to tell you I've loved many times this life and always found a special gem in each and every one, but you, somehow, unlike the rest...stand truly all alone. Its you I love the best of all the loves that I have known. For when I'm next to you there's just no word for how you fill me up.... I overflow and still don't get enough. Each time I try to memorize your face, I just fall into your eyes, I get tangled in your hair. I'm fine across your cheek but near your mouth I grow so weak I think I must lie down. It's

your lips, full, sensuous, god-awful-beautiful, sweet, breathing things that melt me to the ground. I think if I don't kiss then soon, I'll die. Somehow I know that heaven's there...I'm ...just... afraid ... you'll...turn ...away..and then..and then... I think I'm paralyzed
    -FD

IN A MEADOW IN MY MIND

There is a place within my mind where I go and often find a sort of solitary peacefulness. I was lonely here, at first, and vainly searched and longed to find someone to share the lovely things I found and carried there; the warming Sun, the greening things and gentle breeze, the busy clouds, gurgled streams that flickered through dancing leaves, a broken sky of see-through blue, some birds, a bee, a butterfly or two, and on and on......all collected, saved as I had found them on my way.

I love this place, this meadow in my mind, and sadly learned the aching fact that my desire to share this splendid spot, this verdant view, with someone else with loving eyes...could simply not come true. Not for lack of invitation was this made clear to me....I offered many times, but I think the path was too narrow for more than one....I lost them all on the hill above and none ever stayed to reach the grass below.

Then there was you. I don't know from where you came, or where it is you go. I only know the day I came and you were here.... waiting, that you stayed and didn't run as I came near. I choked some tears and turned my head a bit that you might not see, the terrible fear mixed in my joy. I must be wrong. I only 'thought' I saw you there all shining in the light. If I just turned away and looked back, I was sure you'd be gone. No? Still there? I'm surely mad! This cannot be!

Then you turned and looked at me and I knew if I'd gone mad I didn't care...if it took that to be with you.

Your eyes saw deep into my soul, yet I felt not ashamed, just warmed and sweetly raptured in the loving shelter of your mind. And then somehow, I knew I knew you...I've always known you. Around your neck a silver chain, a golden key that fits my heart...when did I lose that? So long ago, I don't recall. But yes, I know you now...the other half my secret soul.

How I long to touch you, to look into your eyes until this disbelief has faded from my mind forever. Then to dare to touch your lips and never have to stop to breathe until the knots tied 'round my choking heart are loosed and fall away and leave me free to worship you for just one small eternity......here in the meadow in my mind.

But if I reach to touch and find no solid thing, a wisp of mist, an insubstantial puff of thought, why then I fear that I shall perish too. I think today I have not got the recklessness to risk it...perhaps tomorrow. I'll think on it tonight.

FD-

PAPER LOVE

Before today you were just a poet's dream,
A flower made of words,
Inky marks on ivory sheets,
My reverential mystic muse,
My dearest hope,
A dreamed uncertain desperate wish,
Angelic twirls of wanting wrapped in midnight smoke,
All yesterday.
But now is different...now is new.
Today is here
And no day shall be again as it was before.
You are no more my paper love.
I have touched you and you are real.
How long I agonized,
Pushed back the burning need
To touch and draw you near.
How many times did I stand so close?
I could feel the warmth of you.
How many times did I ache to hold you to me?
And let your sunshine thaw the frozen garden of my soul
How bold I felt, at last,
When I could bear the pain no more
And saying I had to hold you...did.
Yes, today I touched you!
Not just a casual touch,
Not a doctor checking bones,
Not a passing friendly shoulder squeeze,
Not a poking pretense people do
(meaning more than they'd admit).
No, I held you,

For the pure need a person has to hold
And know they're being held.
We, neither spoke.
I just held you close....and wanted to forever.
I felt you breathing,
Felt the softness of your curls upon my skin,
Felt too, the gentle rhythm of your heart upon my breast,
Oh, sweet heart,
Oh, gentle thing,
Oh, magic,
Oh, splendid creature,
Oh, soft mouth still untouched,
Oh, heaven!
Is there more to life to want than this just now,
Being here, and holding you?
This will do...for here and now.
It will do!
FD-

BEAUTY-BOUND

A tender, gentle, loving man.
A man who loves the harmony in things
But knows the need of standing firm
Against the sometimes-fickle winds
That blow a ship about in troubled seas
A man who seeks out Beauty everywhere
And finds her footsteps in the shifting sands,
The murky shadows of the night,
'Tho he has yet to find her at his side
And know the intimacy of her his soul desires.
His love for her, the one he seeks,
Is born of faith in knowing thins half-seen...
Immense and endlessly profound.
He sees traces of her everywhere:
The regal heraldry of dawn,
The miracle of clouds upon the sky,
The blatant honesty of animals,
The distant majesty of mountains,
The cradling lullaby of meadows in the spring,
The awful awesome artifacts describing her by man,
But most of all she dazzles him to awkwardness,
With her blossom-bursting rhapsody....
That silken sword called" Womanhood".
He knows he's bound to her. Without a choice,
He cannot be but what he is, a Beauty-driven man.
He feels no shame, he is her mount, her steed,
To carry her where're she wills or wishes.
He is hers. All brawling-crude, or delicate-refined.
She needn't even touch him
Just flash a knowing glance

FRANK DALE

And he'd make haste to have it done
In hopes that she would smile at him
Or send him off to heaven with a kiss.
FD-

PEACEFUL LADY

Peaceful Lady of the Western Sea
I'm drawn to you like oceans to the moon.
Your quiet majesty serene,
An exquisite, muted siren's song,
That calls to me across a tranquil sea,
Whose mirror face reflects the sky,
The golden yolk of early dawn,
The purest light of crowning noon,
The amber glow of eventide,
The sapphire shroud of fallen day,
And then...and then...sweet heaven's night,
The crystal specks and diamond sparks,
A silver pearl's cathedral ark.
While down below the currents move,
With patient unrelenting will,
With awesome power and stunning grace,
To stir the blood and steal the hearts
Of those rare souls who search for treasures of the deep.
And I am one......a diver of the depths
Who gathers pearls.
And this is one I found in you.
So now, with love,
I give it back again....to you,
Your Majesty,
My Peaceful Lady of the Western Sea.
FD

IVORY-CREAM

O' fragrant flower ivory-cream
How sharp recalls this lover's dream.
Those tangled twists of auburn curls
Crumpled grass and petaled pearls,
High meadow thick at shade of noon
O' naked earth with azure moon,
Still pounds my heart with touch of thigh,
While look'd on birds where we did lie,
Sweet breath of youth mid-summer bare,
Eternal flames igniting there
Idyllic thrumming throbbing grows,
Sapling dance to breeze that blows,
Moist lips caress soft fuzz and peach,
O' blinding light by arch and breach,
Where rivers rage mild meadow's stream
Volcanic red fades limpid green,
Serenely spent soft moaning sighs,
Fulfilled content for'er to dream,
The sweet embrace of ivory-cream.

FD-

TIME

Most people think that time's a line,
Newton-straight and feather-fine,
But I think not.
I've seen it run so fast you'd swear it's out of breathless
Then crawl so slow you're sure you've witnessed death.
No sir!
There's more to ticking than a clock,
As there's more to clergy than a frock.
It is my studied point of view
Time's both fickle and divine,
It depends completely and precisely
On your current state of mind.

FALLING FOR AMGELS

As I sat one day in murky ponder
I saw an angel flutter by
And with an infant's simple trust
When reaching for the moon
I followed...
Wanting to touch the light.
Beyond all reason
I desired to feel its enchantment
To know the gentle glowing beauty
To somehow hold and be a part of
The ethereal brilliance.
That's ...when I fell.
It was only after reached too far,
Losing my balance,
Knowing the nid-point was passed,
And falling had begun...
Only then could I fully fathom
And know the tragic truth:
That to see is all
'Cause Angels, just like moons,
Are mostly out of reach.
I've never thought it sinful,
Since only I was hurt
By the sinking sadness
Of my isolated fall.
But I wonder,
How Angels look upon
Such pitiful pronation's.

45

How, too, shall I then think on Angels?
O' well!
I guess only time will tell
FD

LADY IN BLACK

How you've haunted me! From first I put my eyes on you. you've never left my mind. The unutterable desire that consumed me then and there was exquisite anguish I knew I'd have to bear each unexpected time I might step into a room or turn a corner and find you there to fabn this fire that blows up bright and showers sparks against the midnight of my mind when I let myself, like now, just sit and think of you...It's too late....I'm done for now! I must go on...I cannot put it down...cannot close the gate as thoughts of you run tearing through my mind...ripping proper thoughts and carefully chosen phrases from their silver-plated pins. In some divinely throttled way my mind's a-mock and will not stop 'til it sorts out all the thoughts f you I've strewn like errant breezes blowing through an orchard in the spring....little perfumed pretty pieces of the picture of the puzzle that is you. I know not where this takes me, but but where it will .... I must. My heart's atremble now...but on I go all dizzied with the thrill!

Lovely Lady dressed in black, what dark and haunting dream is this? Was I asleep? Is this awake? There's little mourning here it seems to me. How soft-spectacular are the richly umbered tones reflecting from the cloth that dance in subtle shadings on the color of your face...the ripened summer-gold of you. What is that smoky thing that hovers there in murky mystifying shadows to tease my eyes and pull my mind within to search for little treasures that linger out of sight....an ethereal inky fog that soft black cloth halos all around you. It is elegant to my eye, a prime thing, a simple basic beauty bit...I know just how to paint that look...as Rubens did I think, glazing ivory black on umber burnt on white. And as if joy of color weren't enough, there's still the troubling form and shape of you......and I've yet to touch upon the world of wind-blown dreams bound up in your hair. How complete you seem to me to be. I know Beauty has many faces and I see that one of them is yours.

Once upon a Spring ago I saw you tightly dressed in April green. How you filled me with thoughts of love and lying in the sun. The things you stirred in me were almost more than I could bear. At last I had to leave that place and wrench you from my mind. Later on I had a better grip and told myself you were not a thing for me to use. And pointedly, in fact, you had to be some other person's Muse. If only you were mine! How tender I would be! How softly would I touch you but I think its not to be.
And later on, I saw you several times...once I even dared some words...they weren't much and didn't serve me very well. I thought to tell

you of my life-long search for Beauty that it might strike a chord and let you know I'd found you out, but that's not the way it went at all. You remarked that such a quest revealed a shallow mind. So, I was crushed, of course, for quite the longest time. Then you were gone.... somewhere out of sight...but never out of mind.

Now you're back again to haunt me once again, more lovely than before. There's a phantom feral feline prowling deep inside of you that makes me want to hold and stroke it, feel the static of its fur, to feel it stretch all rapt and wrapping, to listen to it purr.

What am I left to do? You are everywhere I turn: I look up from my work and see you standing there just doing what you do; but once you're in my eyes you fill the center of my mind.

Oh, Haunting Lovely Lady, Magic Dressed in Black, what I'd give to see love glowing in your eyes...and think that its for me. But since you're someone else's Muse it's just a thing that cannot be...but its the thing I'd dearly wish for…. if the wishing's left to me

FD-

THE YES OF SPRING

This day's just a moment in time,
The equinox of Spring.
And they say that Spring's
A promise always kept.
I say further that love's
The 'yes' os Spring
And so, to you and Spring
I say yes, yes, yes.!
Let the blooming show begin!
FD

THE END

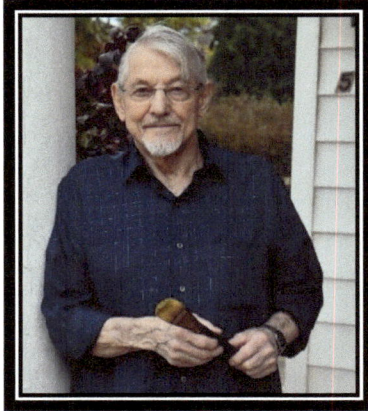

ABOUT THE AUTHOR

Born in the middle of the Great Depression Frank Dale spent much of his early years traveling as his family searched for job opportunities throughout the war years of the 1940's. After enduring many operations recovering from a childhood accident, he went to high school in Northern California and started college. His schooling was interrupted by a marriage which set him upon an odyssey of many jobs and skills. After a divorce, a remembered love, and his dedication to his artistic skills he decided to live alone, teach art, and paint all the Vermeers.

www.ingramcontent.com/pod-product-compliance
Lightning Source LLC
Chambersburg PA
CBHW041523090426

42737CB00037B/18